Cycle Chase

The Championship Season

Written by C. J. Naden

Troll Associates

Photo credits: Mary Grothe, Daytona International Speedway, Dozier
Mobley, Cycle Guide

The start of a long racing season.

It's like the Super Bowl and the World Series, the Olympic Gold Medal and the Triple Crown. But in the world of professional motorcycle racing, it could be called "the chase." They all mean the same thing—the tops in the sport, the best there is.

A tough schedule lies ahead.

The best in American motorcycle racing is the National Motorcycle Championship Series. It begins in February and ends in October. That means nine months and more than twenty races. It means danger and skill and speed and luck. But when it's over, if you've won, it also means the top.

Home away from home on the circuit.

National Championship races are held at many different circuits. The pro tour may wind back and forth from California to New Hampshire, from Florida to Pennsylvania. It means a lot of traveling for riders, mechanics, and equipment. It is a long, tiring schedule, and many people take part in the chase to the top.

Bikes are pushed out on the track at race time.

Championship races are run by the American Motorcycle Association. Riders race for points as well as prize money. The rider with the most points at the end of the season is the National Champion. Besides the largest share of the prize money, the champion will race all next season with a big number "1" painted on the winning cycle.

Novices carry red racing numbers.

The AMA approves thousands of races each year for Novices and Experts. To become a Novice, you must be at least 16 years old. After a certain number of victories as a Novice, you are classified as an Expert. And that means you can join the chase for the pro title.

Leaning out of a sidecar on the turns.

You must be an Expert to race on the national circuit. Why? Because these races are tough, dangerous, and only for the best. You must be able to handle many kinds of motorcycles. They are all different. Some cycles are built for dirt-track racing, others for road races. And you must be able to ride in different kinds of events.

"Leathers" protect against injury in a fall.

Motorcycles used in professional races may look a lot like those ridden on public highways. But they are different in many ways. The pro bikes are highly tuned and fitted with special brakes, shocks, and other parts. Riders must wear proper safety equipment—approved helmets with face covers or goggles, boots, and leather clothing.

A must—bike inspection before each race.

Pro riders compete in four different types of Championship races—enduros, moto-cross events, oval-track races, and road races. Enduros are held on natural terrain. Moto-cross events are held on closed, rugged courses. Oval-track races are held on flat, dirt tracks. And road races are held on paved road courses.

Waiting for the start—rain or shine.

Early motorcycle races were called Tourist Trophy races. The first one was held in 1907 on the Isle of Man. Motorcycle races are still held on that small English island. American motorcycle racing began in 1903. The bikes raced on the same tracks as automobiles. In some places, they still do. And in all kinds of weather!

Major events attract the fans.

Motorcycle racing is a very popular sport, with big prize money for the top riders. Fans flock by the thousands to Championship events. The opener of the Championship season can easily draw more than 50,000 people. They come to cheer their favorite riders in their roaring, snorting machines.

Rider against rider, bike against bike.

Both riders and motorcycles race for points. The make of cycle
with the most points over the season earns the Manufacturer's
Championship, a highly prized award. So, in any Championship
race, both riders and bikes are competing against each other.

Women riders are part of the pro ranks.

The season may open with the Daytona 200—a road race at Daytona International Speedway in Florida. It attracts riders —both male and female—from all over the world. The 320-kilometer (200-mile) race requires riders to shift gears and use brakes at the tight corners. It is a great test of skill for the pros.

Riding close and fast on the turns.

The big cycles at Daytona have up to six operating speeds and large gas tanks. There is plenty of action as the fast racing bikes zoom along at high speeds. Most of the time, the top riders are breathing down each other's necks. One spill could eliminate many machines. And sometimes it does.

International racing action at Daytona.

The Daytona 200 is the most important race of the Championship season. It is also the best-known motorcycle race in the United States. The winner earns big prize money, points, glory, and worldwide fame.

Heading for a win.

At one time, most road races were run on public highways that were closed to regular traffic for these events. Today most road races take place on specially designed, closed, paved courses such as Daytona. The Speedway combines an oval-shaped track with a flat road course in the infield area.

Approaching a twisting infield turn.

In their bright helmets and racing leathers, these riders speed along the straightaways at more than 280 kilometers an hour (175 miles an hour). But they must slow down for the twisting roads of the infield. This is where the riders need the greatest skill. And this is what makes Daytona so tough. You can't win on speed alone.

Charging around a sweeping turn.

Excitement starts early after the green "go" flag. Crouching low over their roaring machines, the riders zoom into the first left bend in a noisy pack. They are almost close enough to touch each other. But at these speeds, that's the one thing they don't want to do!

Before and after a race, the
pit area is an exciting place.
Curious cycle fans and photog-
raphers mill about, talking with
racing crews and taking pic-
tures. But during the race, there
will be excitement of a different
kind. A good pit crew can re-
fuel a racing cycle in as little as
six seconds!

Headed for victory.

All riders must obey the flag signals during a race. A green flag
starts the race. Yellow means danger on the track. Red means
stop—go back to the starting line. Yellow and red-striped means
oil on the track—always dangerous in a race. But if you're out
in front, what you want to see is the black-and-white checkered
flag. It means "the winner!"

Away goes the bike!

To win, the pros have to keep their cycles in top condition. Their lives depend on such things as good brakes and tires. Good tires grip the road on curves. But sometimes—good tires or not—the rider leans too far, and bike and rider part company!

Flat out on the course.

In a road race, speed is the key to victory. Riders want to get as much speed out of their cycles as they possibly can. So each rider ducks down low over the bike. This is called "flat out." It cuts down on wind resistance, and helps build up maximum speed.

Taking a turn on a dirt track.

Road races are held on paved roads. But oval-track races are held on dirt tracks called "flat tracks." When going into a turn, each rider uses one foot for balance, and "slides" the bike around the corners. Dragging a shoe on the track would wear it out very quickly. So each rider wears a steel-bottomed boot, called a "skid shoe."

Too close for mistakes.

Road-racing cycles are faster than oval-track cycles. In a road race, riders do not drag their feet on the turns. The cyclists lean their bikes into the sharp corners. There is very little room for error. The riders know that, and so do the fans. That's what makes a road race so exciting and so popular.

Leaning into a dangerous turn.

The turns are the most dangerous spots in any cycle race. All it takes is one error in judgment for the rider to suddenly lose control, and go skidding off the course. That's one reason why professional riders wear safety helmets, racing leathers, and gloves.

Racing into the darkness.

Some road races last as long as six hours. Two riders are needed for each cycle in these events. The riders take turns handling the bike. Each turn may last anywhere from one to three hours. Sometimes these races don't end until sundown.

At the starting line.

The start of a Championship road race is one of motorcycle racing's most thrilling moments. The riders line up on the narrow track. They bend forward over their noisy machines, eyes ahead, hands sure and steady. One hand is on the clutch lever, the other is ready to twist the throttle. The air crackles with excitement!

The race for the lead.

The green flag—go! The bikes roar down the straightaway and around the turn, leaving nothing but noise and smoke behind them. The deafening sound of the fierce, snarling engines drowns out the wild noise of the cheering crowd. In a blur of color, the riders fight and jockey for position.

Leaning just far enough.

Nearing the turn, each cyclist leans at a sharp, dangerous angle. Far enough, but not too far. The angle must be just right on every turn. If it is even a little too sharp, the knee of the cyclist's racing leathers may scrape the pavement. The secret is leaning just far enough.

Streaking out ahead.

Around that first turn, the riders pour on the speed once again. Then one machine leaps out of the pack and streaks ahead. The leader's racing number stands out against its white background. The crowd recognizes the number and starts to cheer as the bike whizzes past.

The winners!

Victory is what all cycle riders want—whether they are Novices or Experts, beginners or pros. What a thrill it is to cross the finish line first and hear the crowds cheering for you. And when you get that gleaming trophy in victory lane, you know you're the best.